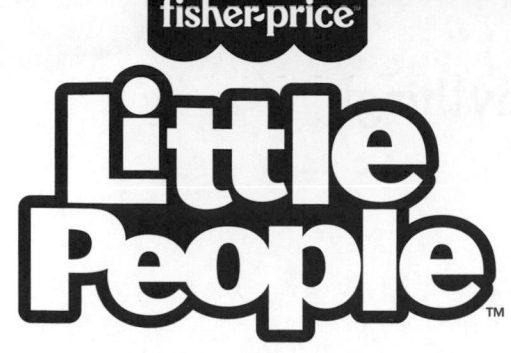

fisher-price
Little People ™

MY BIG COLORING BOOK

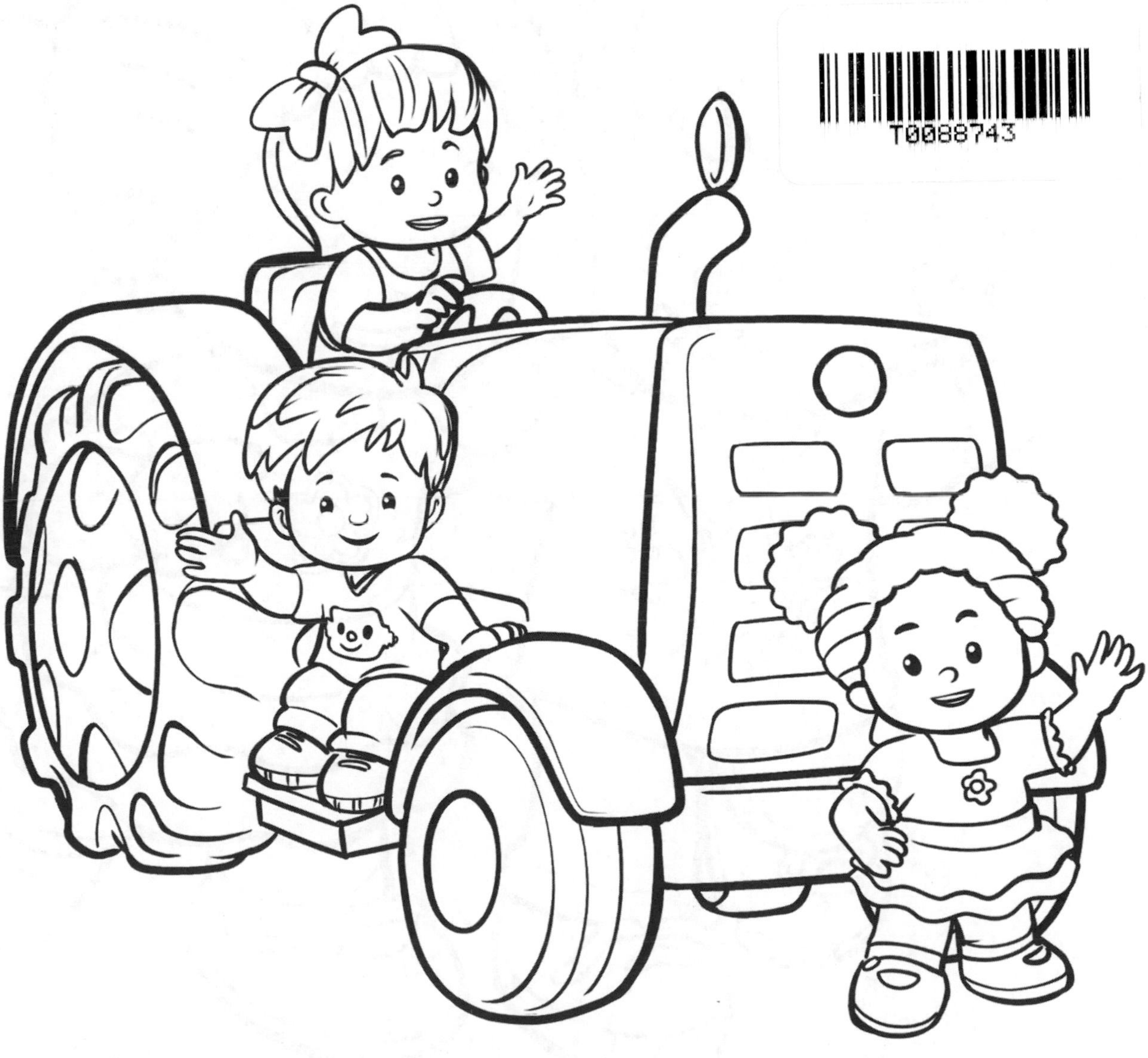

BuzzPoP

Say "Hello!" to Eddie.

Play inside the pretty house.

Do you like to read books?

Mia has a pet rabbit. Do you have any pets?

Can you feed the kitten?

Do you like video games?

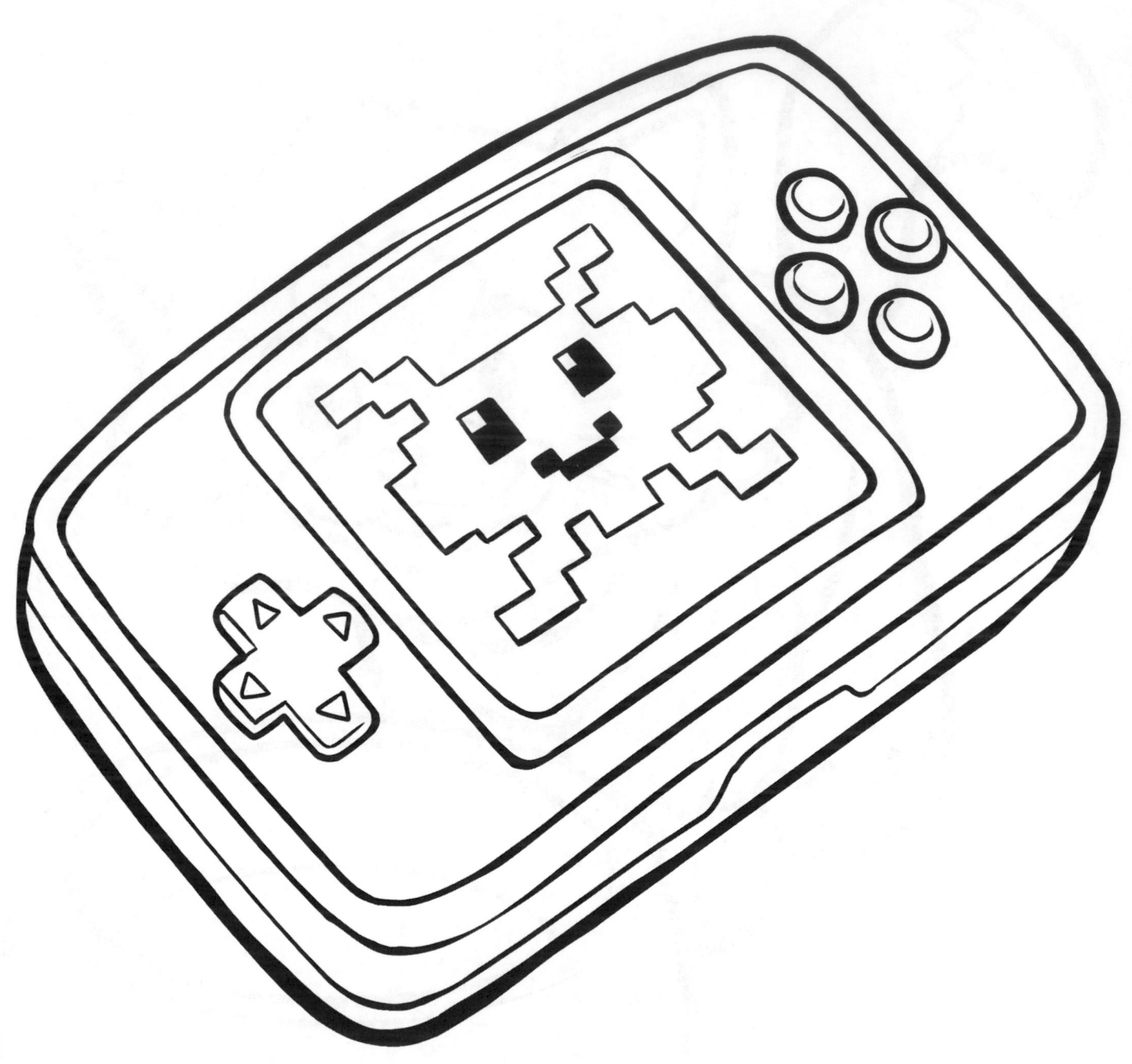

What's your favorite video game to play?

Do you like to stack blocks?

Can you count the radios on this page?

Hello, babies!

Shh! The baby is sleeping.

Do you like surprises?
Color in this big present.

Hold on tight to these balloons
so they don't fly away.

Do you wear glasses?

Can you color this dress in your favorite color?

Drinking hot chocolate on a cold day
will make you feel warm.

This bus takes kids to school.

Teachers help students learn.

Sofie loves doing math!

Do you know how to play the piano?

Circle the French horn that is different from the others.

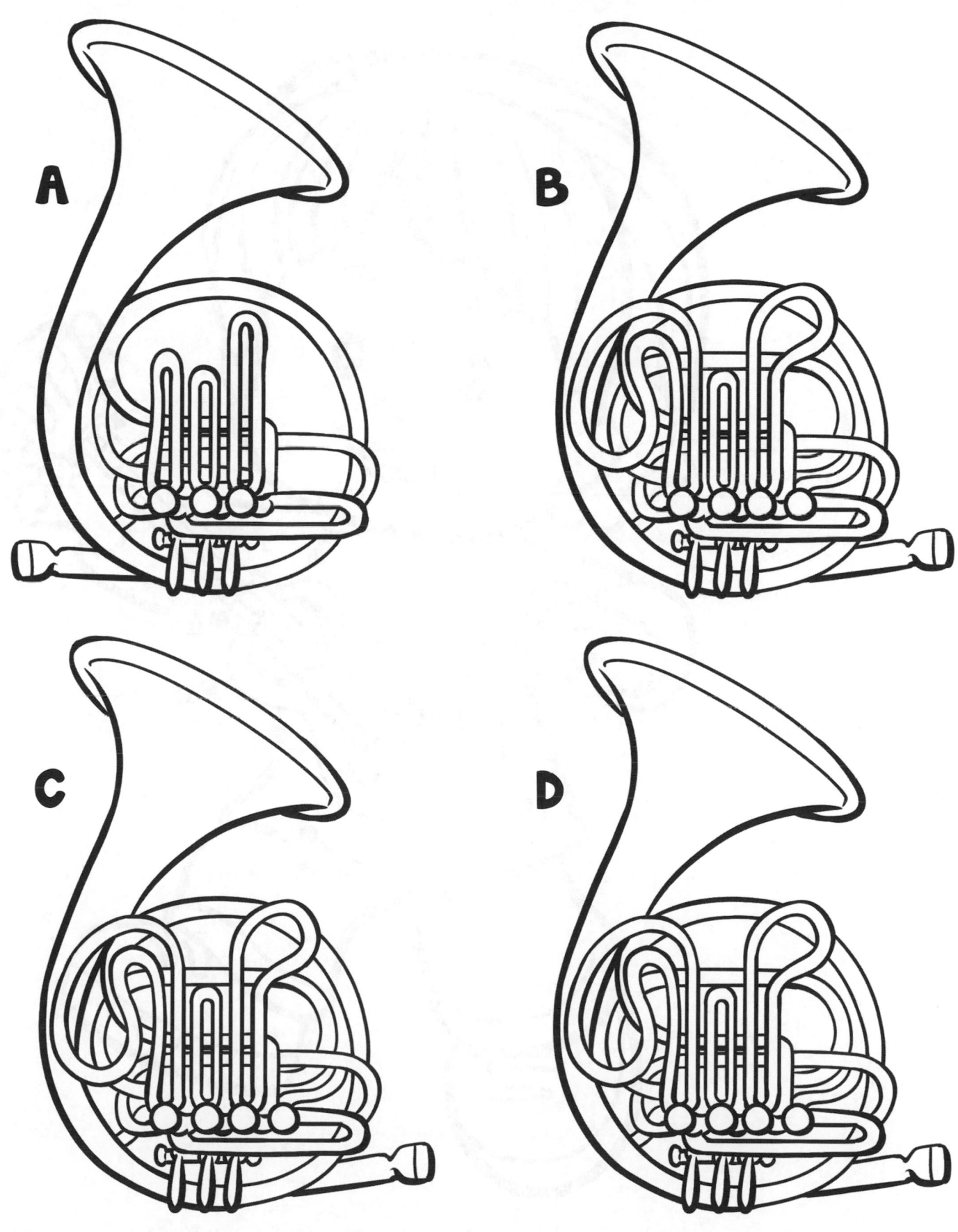

Can you name the instrument? Connect the dots!

Can you color this guitar green?

Do you want to play the clarinet?

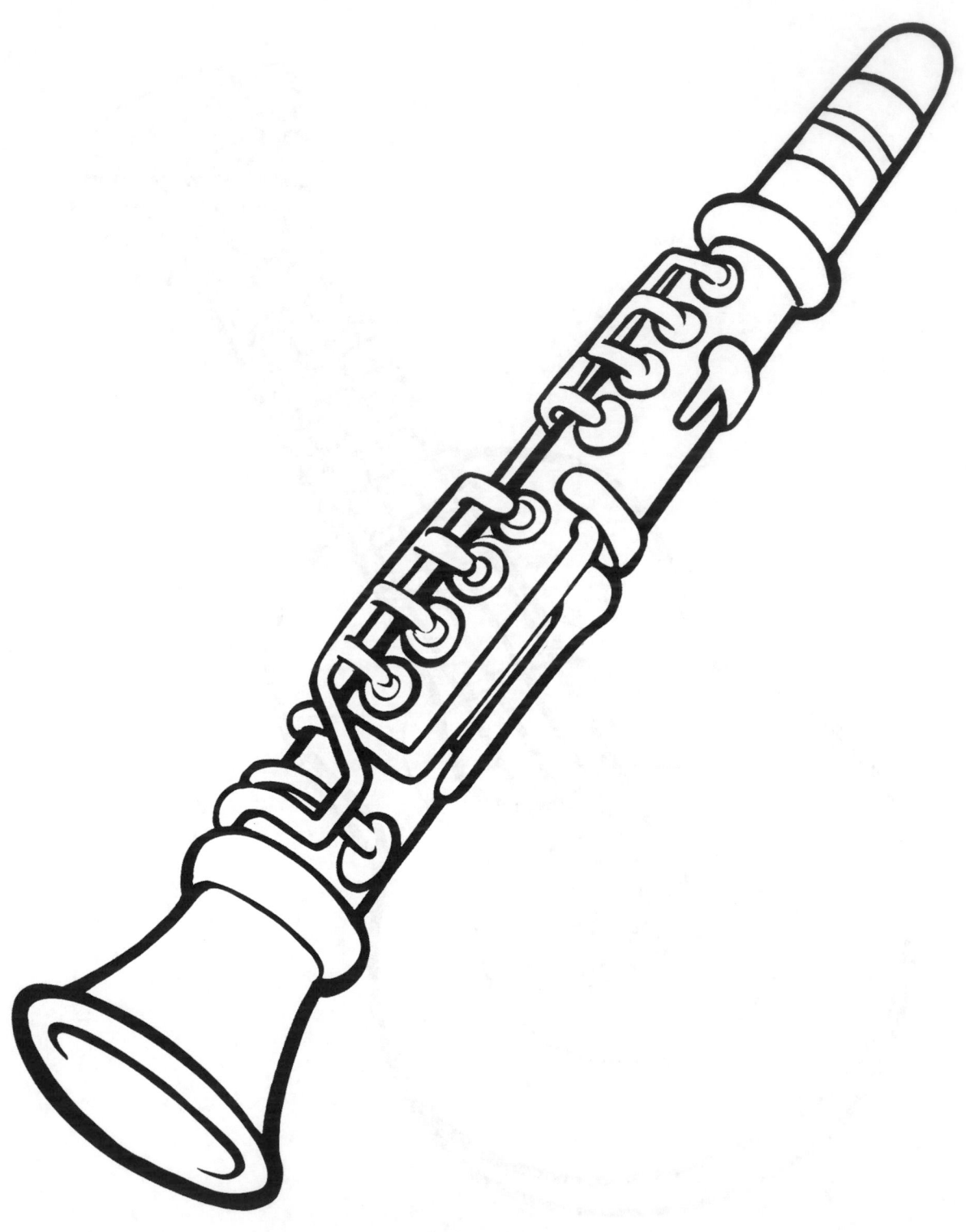

You can play music on the saxophone.

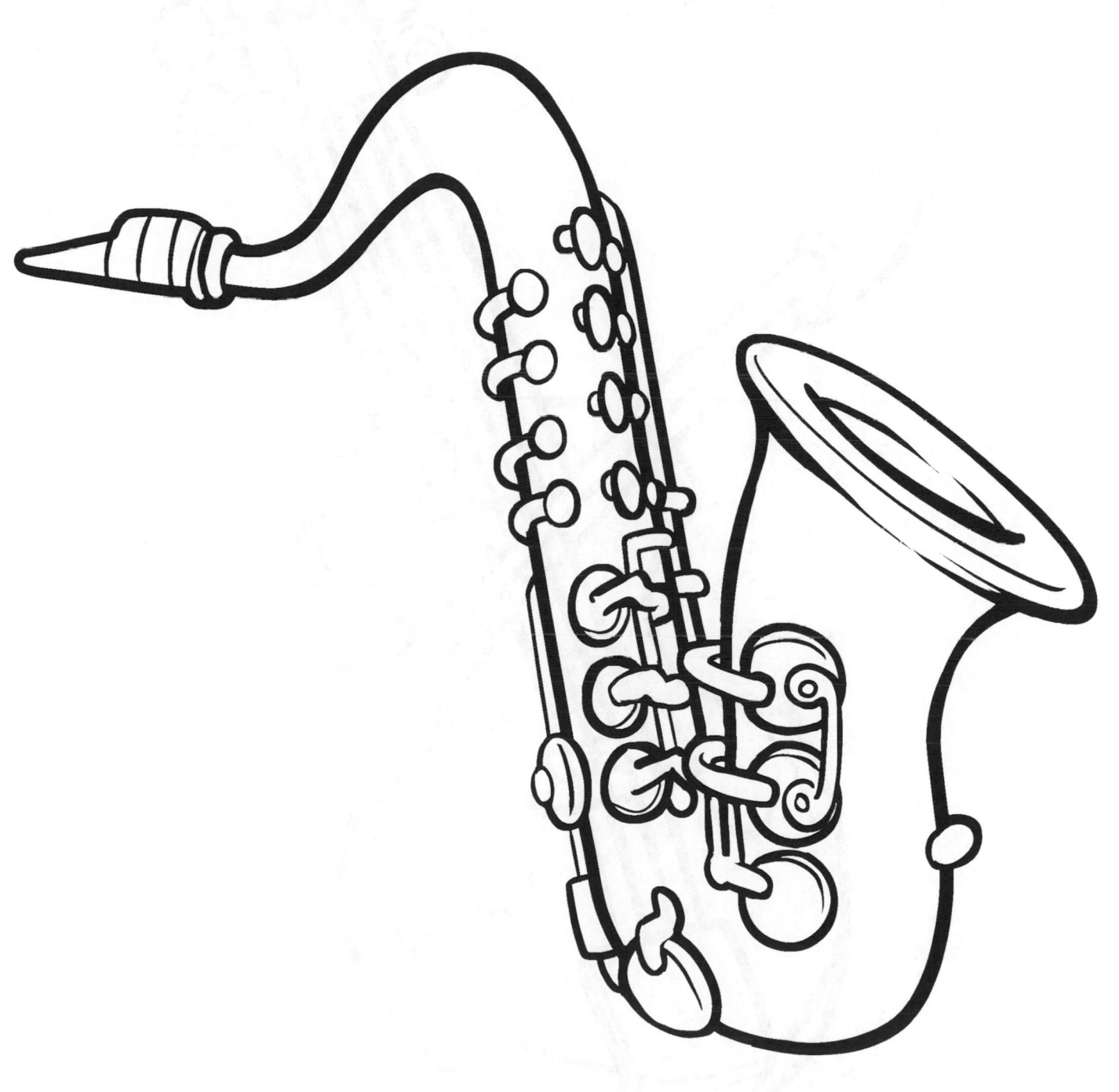

Play a violin with a bow.

How many flutes do you see?

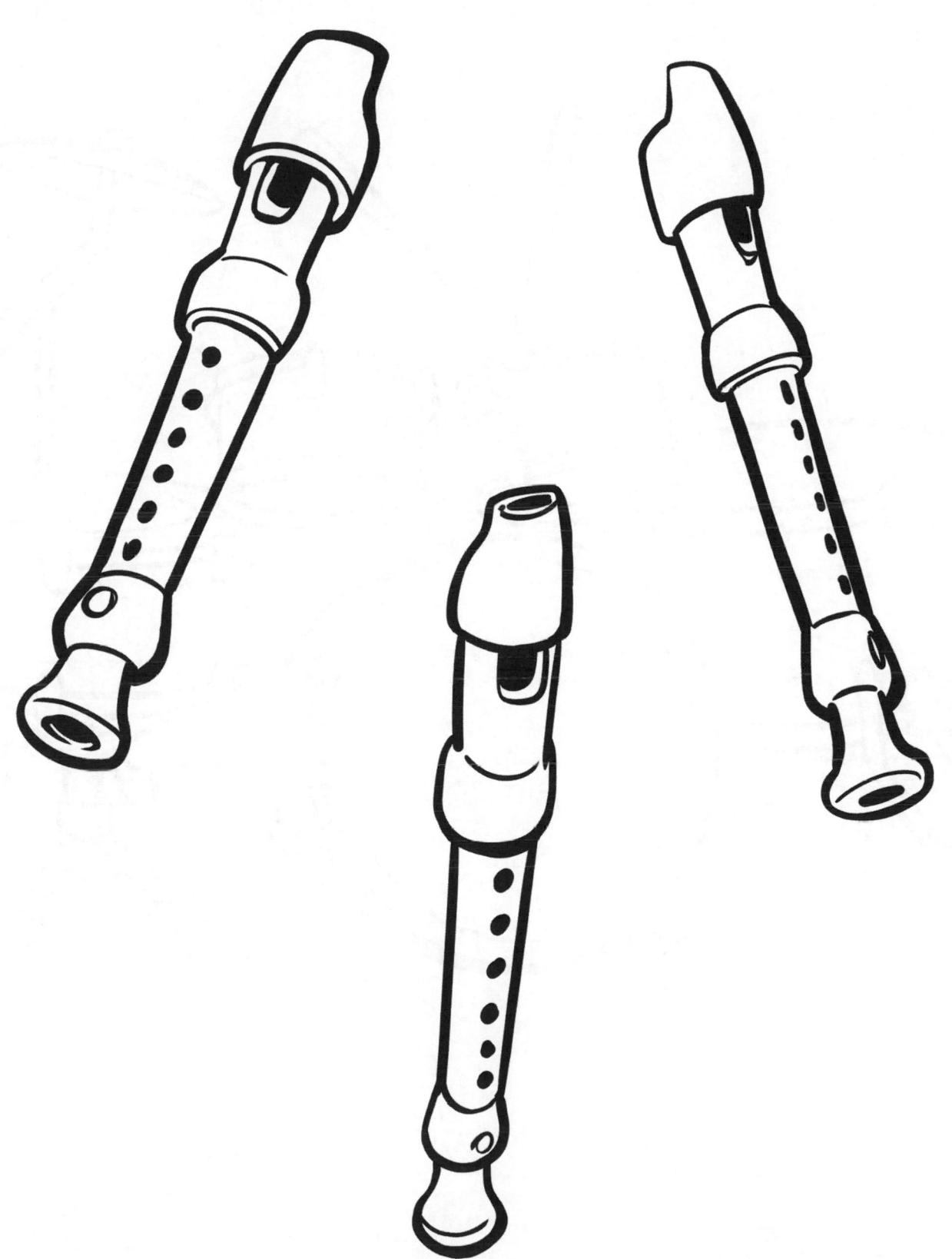

Use drumsticks to bang on this drum set.

This bear plays the drums.

Tessa, Eddie, and Koby each want to sing.
Follow the path to find out who will get the microphone today.

Trumpets are loud instruments.

Cellos have four strings.

Some adults wear ties to work.
Can you draw spots on his tie?

What do you want to be when you grow up?
How about an astronaut?

Rocket ships fly into space.

Telescopes stand on tripods.

Planets and stars can be found in space.

Circle the planet that is different from the others.

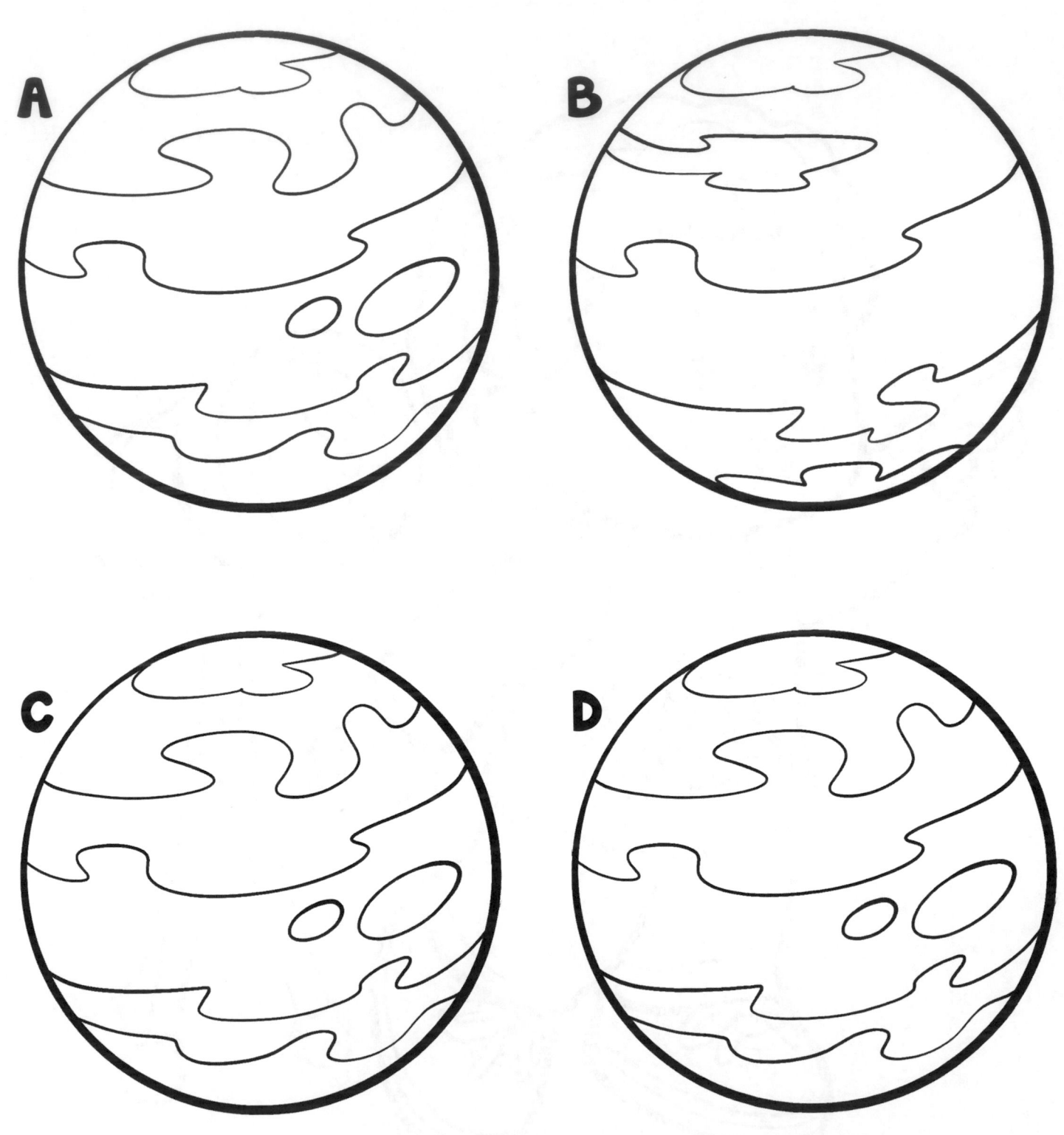

Sofie is a great problem-solver.

This police car flashes its red lights.

Judge Tessa calls the court to order.

An ambulance takes sick people to the hospital.

Doctors can help you feel better
when you're sick or hurt.

Eddie wants to be a nurse.

Dentists clean and fix teeth.

The mail carrier delivers mail to your home.

Sofie wants to be a veterinarian to help animals.

Race car drivers wear helmets!

Vroom! This car goes fast!

Mechanics can fix cars.

Use your favorite colors to decorate this car.

What do you like to eat?
Draw your favorite food on the clipboard below.

Do you like to eat tacos?

Waiters bring people food in restaurants.

Eddie is a cashier at a grocery store.

Juice boxes are tasty.

What do you like to eat in your sandwich?

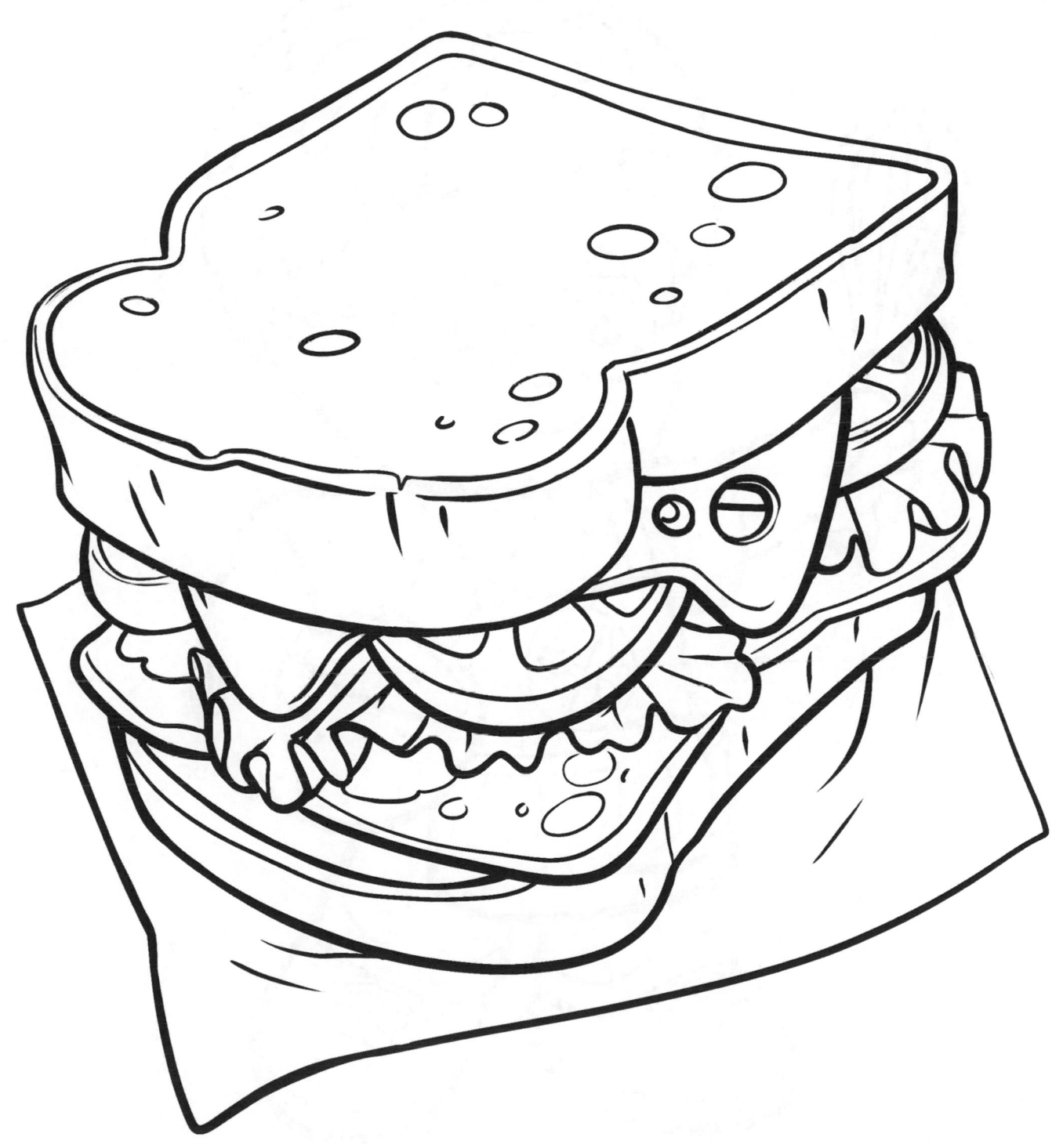

Bakers mix ingredients to make breads and pastries.

Which path leads to the cake?

Circle the cupcake that is different from the others.

A

B

C

D

Connect the dots to reveal the sweet treat.

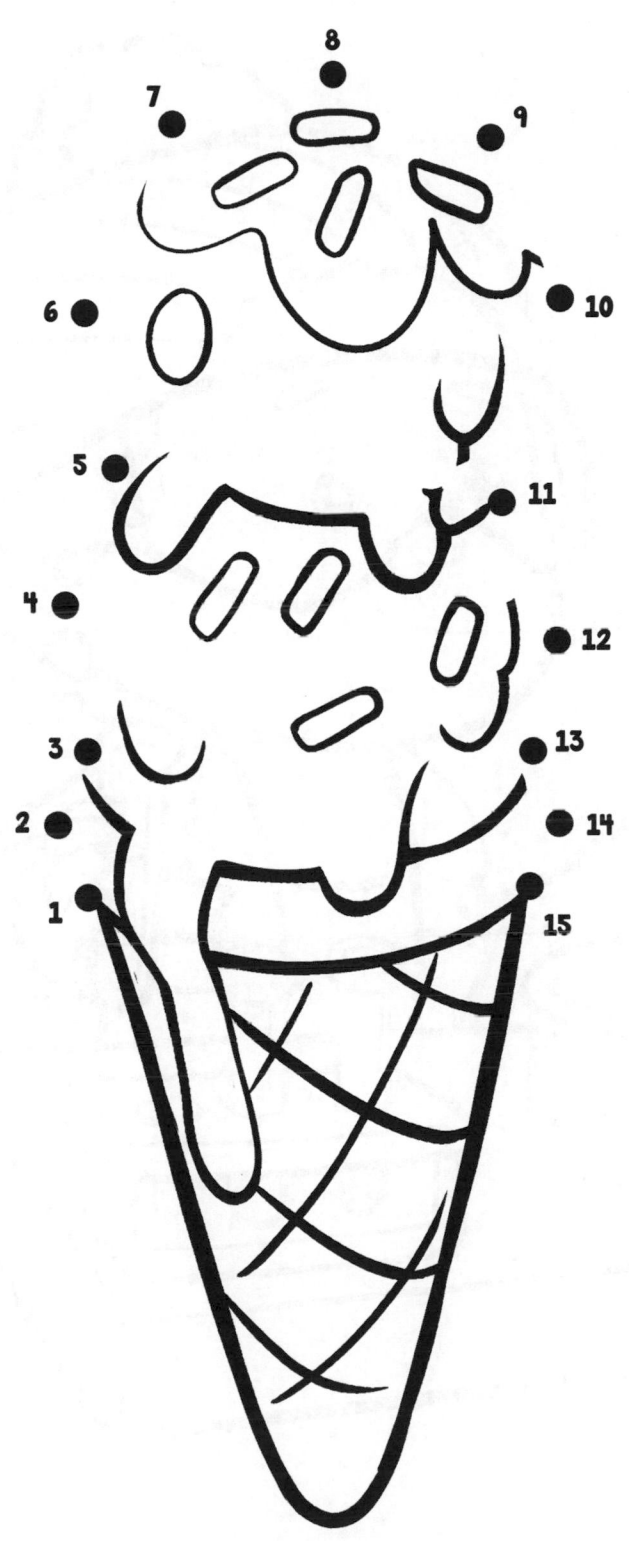

Some scientists mix chemicals in test tubes.

Programmers work with computers.

What vehicle makes the noise "choo choo"?
Connect the dots!

Koby can't wait to go outside.

Put on your shoes before you go outside.

The sun is shining bright today.

It's a beautiful day. Let's go play!

Will you put on a performance on this stage?

Play, learn, and grow in the tree house!

Mia and Sofie play astronomer in the tree house.

Can you ride a bicycle?

These shiny roller skates are brand-new!

Do you ride in a stroller?

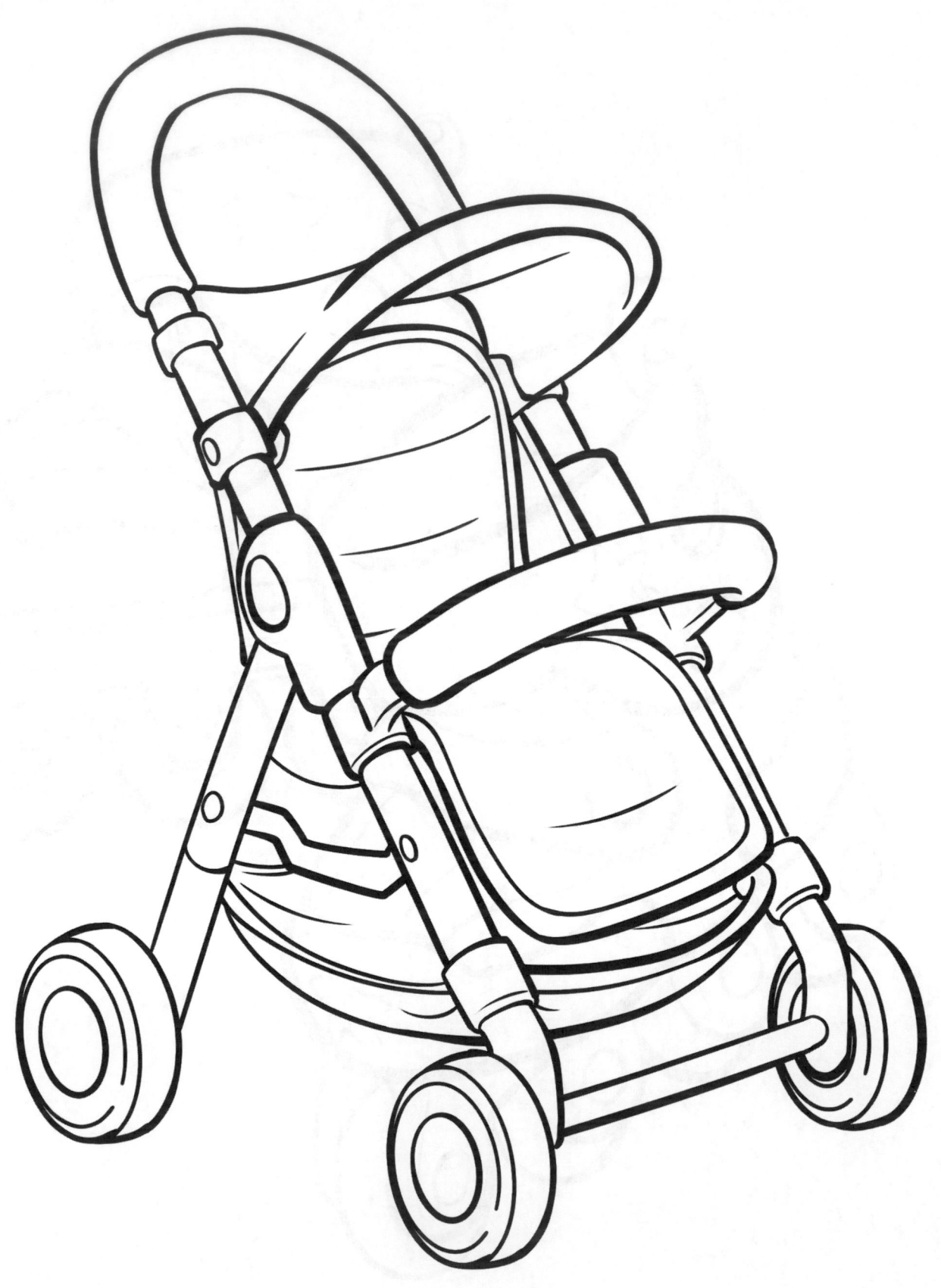

Color this wagon red.

Tessa rides her scooter fast, fast, fast.

Eddie likes to fly kites.

Jumping rope is healthy and fun!

Koby can juggle.

Tessa swings on the tire.

Will you play with this puppy?

Puppy kisses!

Mia is running with the puppy.

Koby, Mia, and Sofie are racing. Who will win the trophy?
Follow the path to find out.

Can you match the equipment for each sport?

A

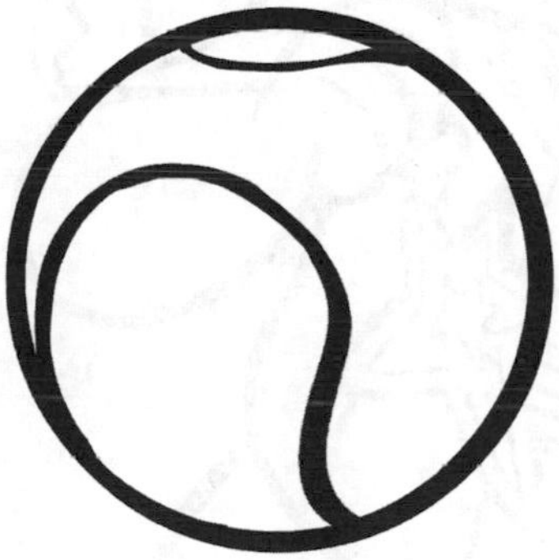

B

C

1

2

3

What's your favorite sport?

Can you count the soccer balls on this page?

A trip to the beach is a fun way to spend a hot day!

Don't forget to pack these items for the beach.
Match the images to the correct shadows.

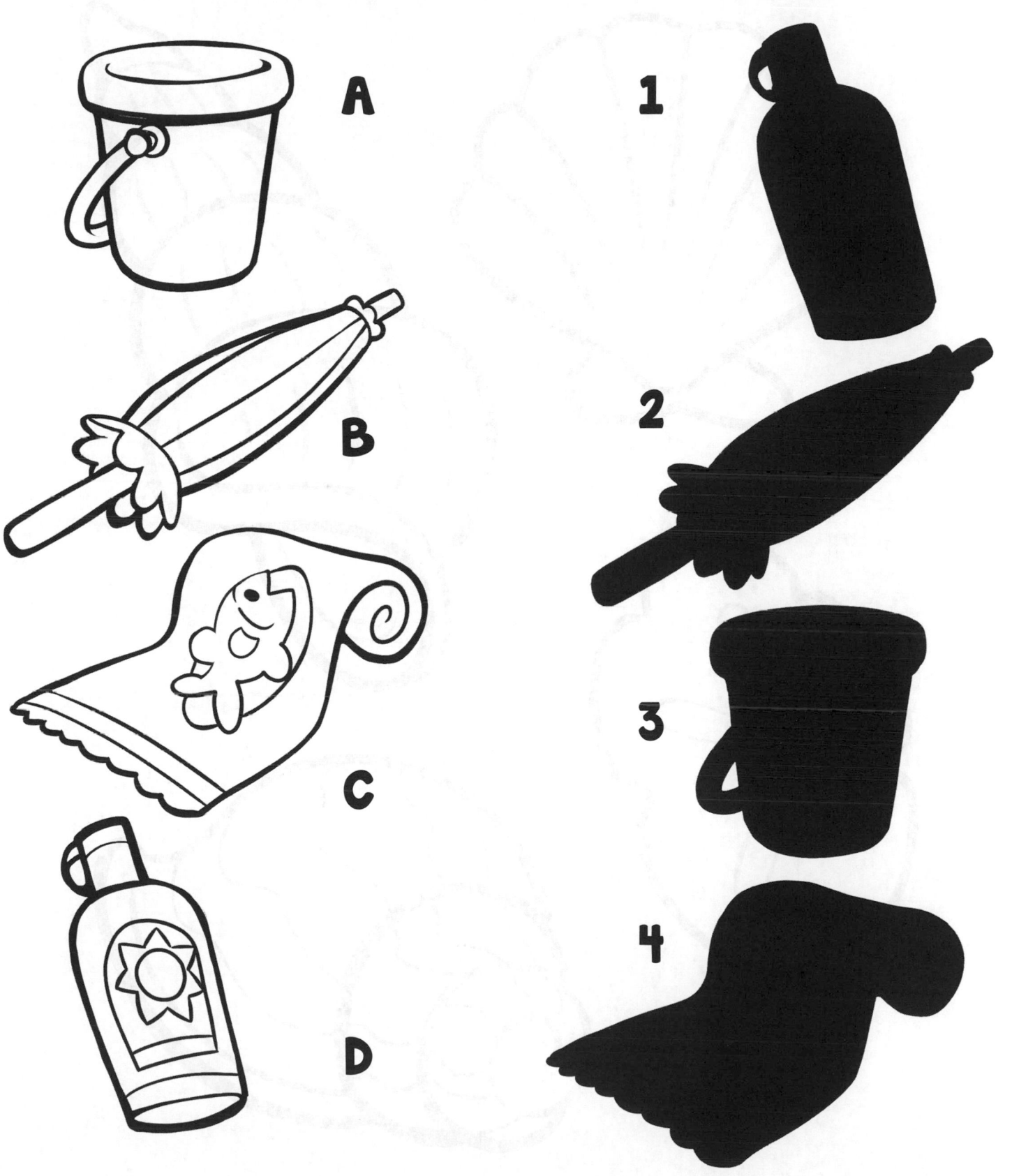

A

B

C

D

1

2

3

4

You can collect seashells at the beach.

Tessa is playing with a beach ball.

A sweater will keep you warm when it's cold outside.

You can build a snowman on a snowy day.

This rainbow appeared after the rain stopped.

Mia plays by her own rules.

Eddie loves to dress up.

Mia is a princess.

This pirate is hunting for treasure.

The treasure chest is filled with gold.

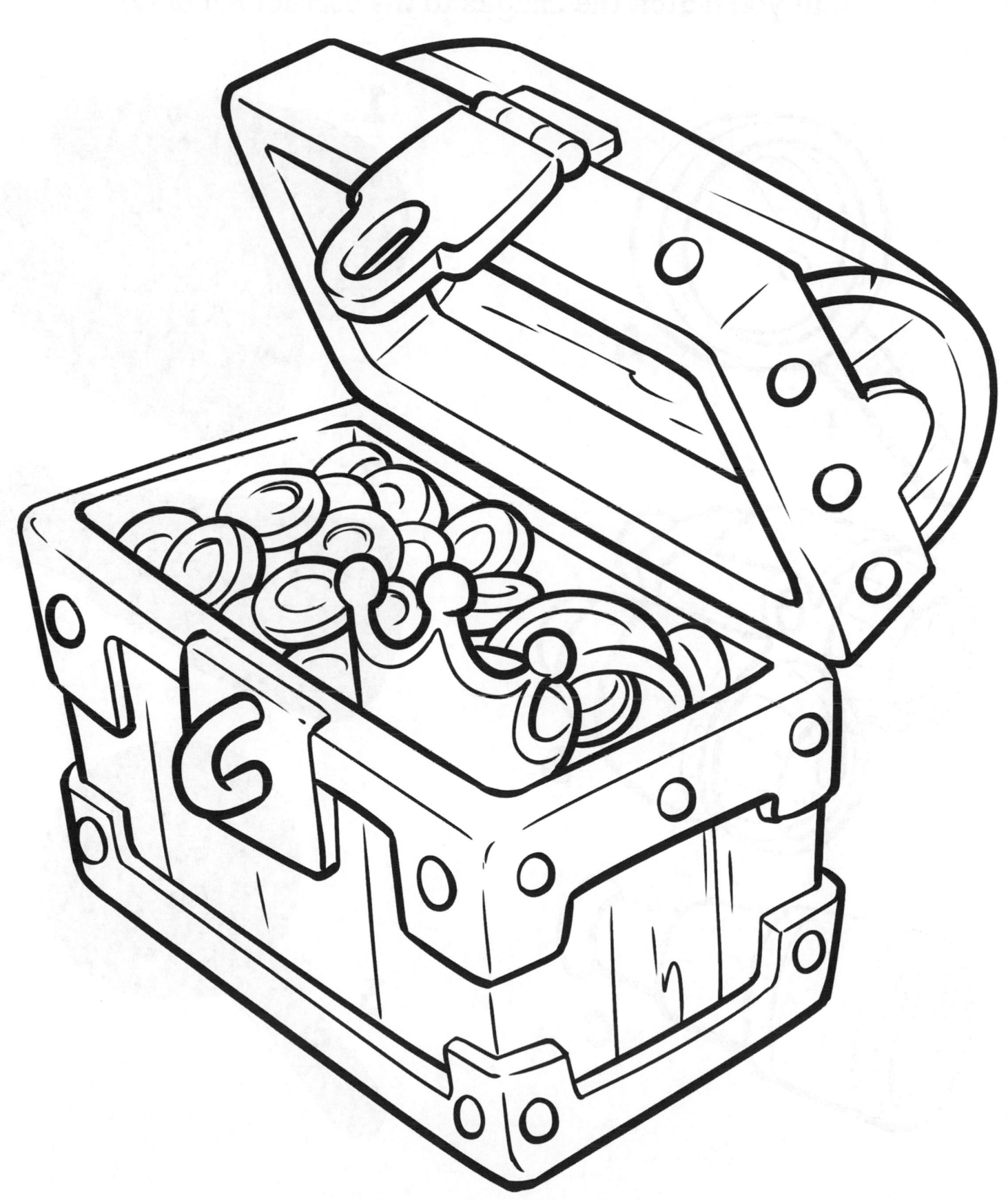

Magnifying glasses, binoculars, and telescopes give you a closer look.
Can you match the images to the correct shadows?

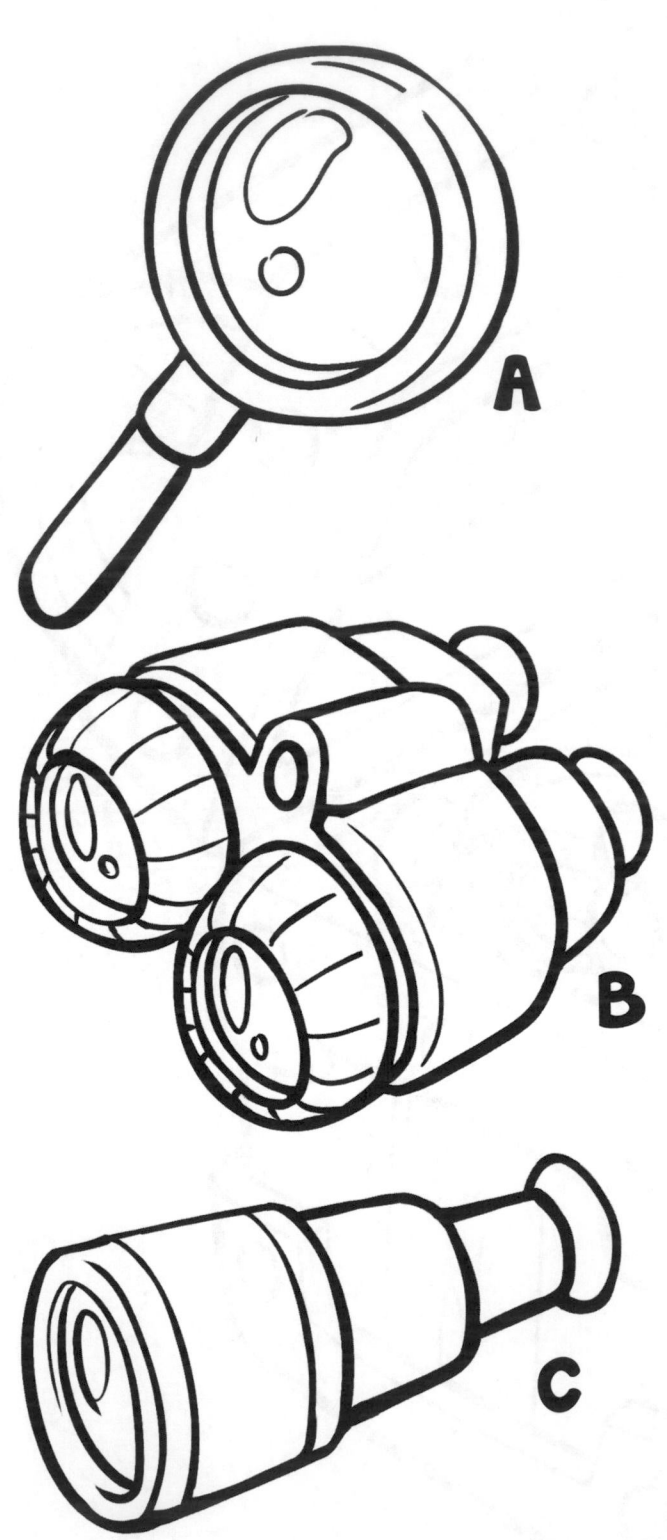

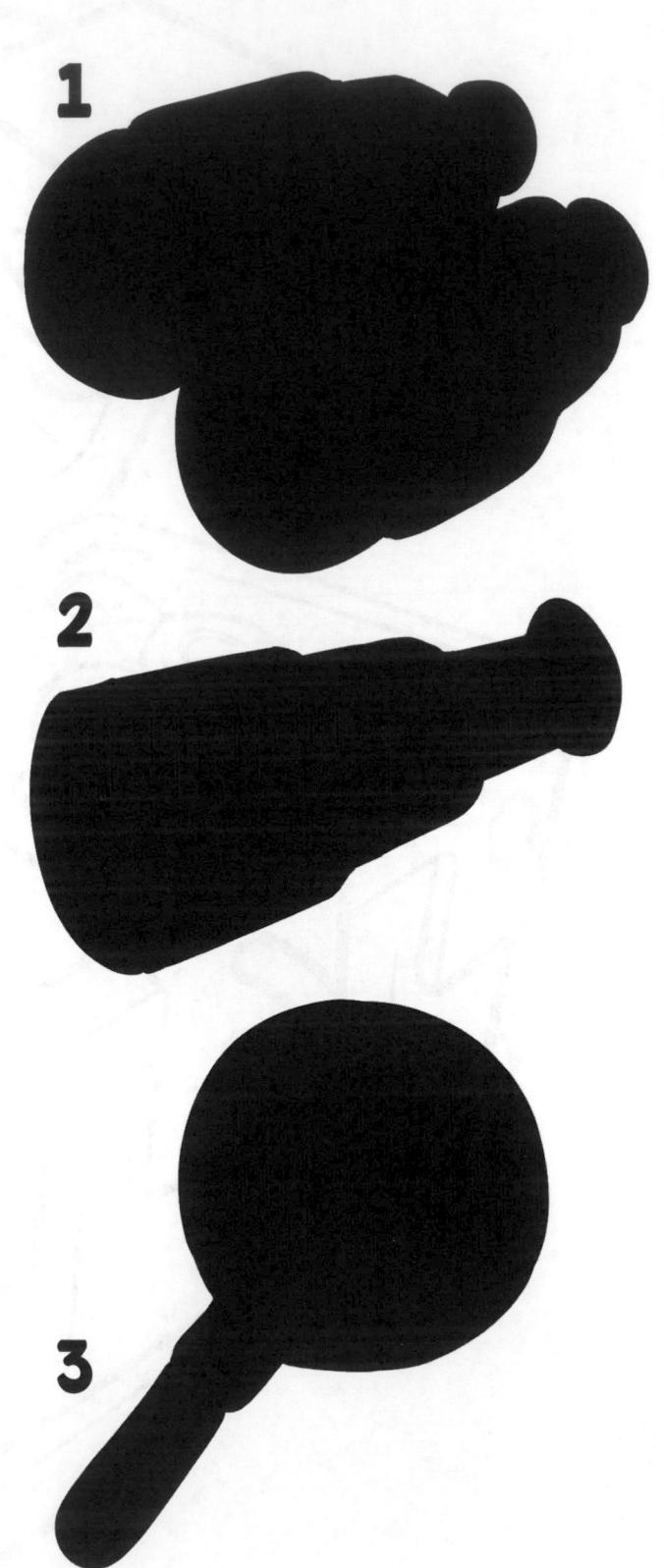

Sofie uses a magnifying glass to find a clue.

Talk into the megaphone to make your voice louder.

Photographers take photos with their cameras.

Use a paintbrush to mix colors.

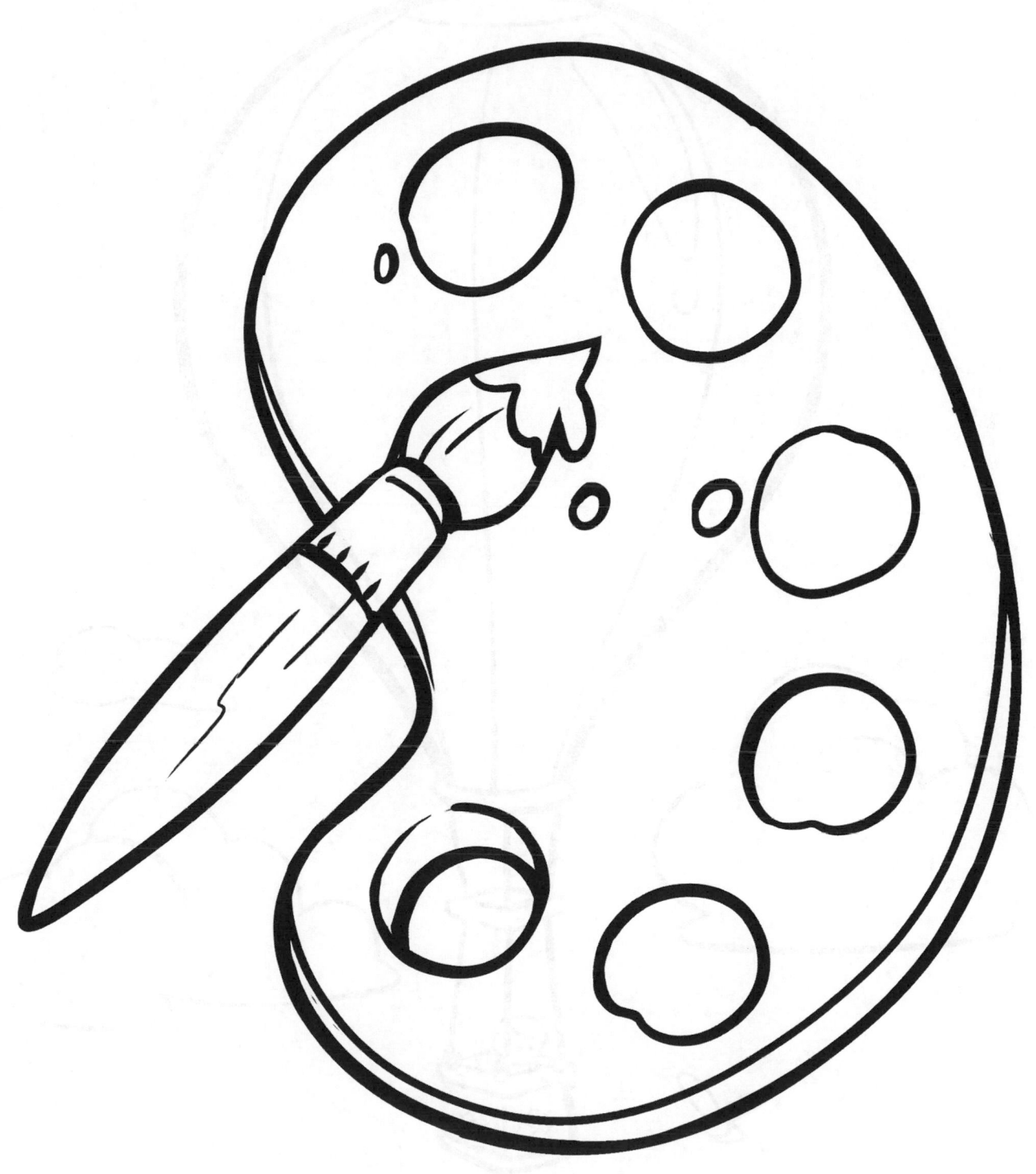

This hot-air balloon flies high in the sky.
What do you see below?

Mia welcomes you to her farm.

A hat keeps the sun out of Koby's eyes.

Can you color this fence blue?

Can you count the flowers on this page?

These pots are empty.
Can you fill them with flowers?

Can you color these tulips purple?

The sails on the windmill go round and round.

Tractors can be used to plant crops.

The garbage truck takes trash to the dump.

A bulldozer can scoop up dirt.

This man drives trucks.

Who is in the barnyard?

This peacock shows off his feathers.

What animal says "neigh"? Connect the dots!

A mother horse watches over her foal.

This cow grazes in the sunlight.

Circle the cow that is different from the others.

A

B

C

Llamas help keep sheep safe on the farm.

This sheep is happy.

Turtles live in water.

Tortoises live on land.

Tortoises move slowly.

This chicken is crossing the road.

This bunny eats carrots as a special treat.
Which path leads to the carrots?

A **B** **C**

Color this parrot's wings orange.

Birds lay eggs.

Birds call, "tweet, tweet, tweet!"

These mice are eating cheese.

Mice eat fifteen to twenty times a day.

Ducks say "quack!"

Color each butterfly a different color.

Can you identify these bugs?
Match the images to the correct shadows.

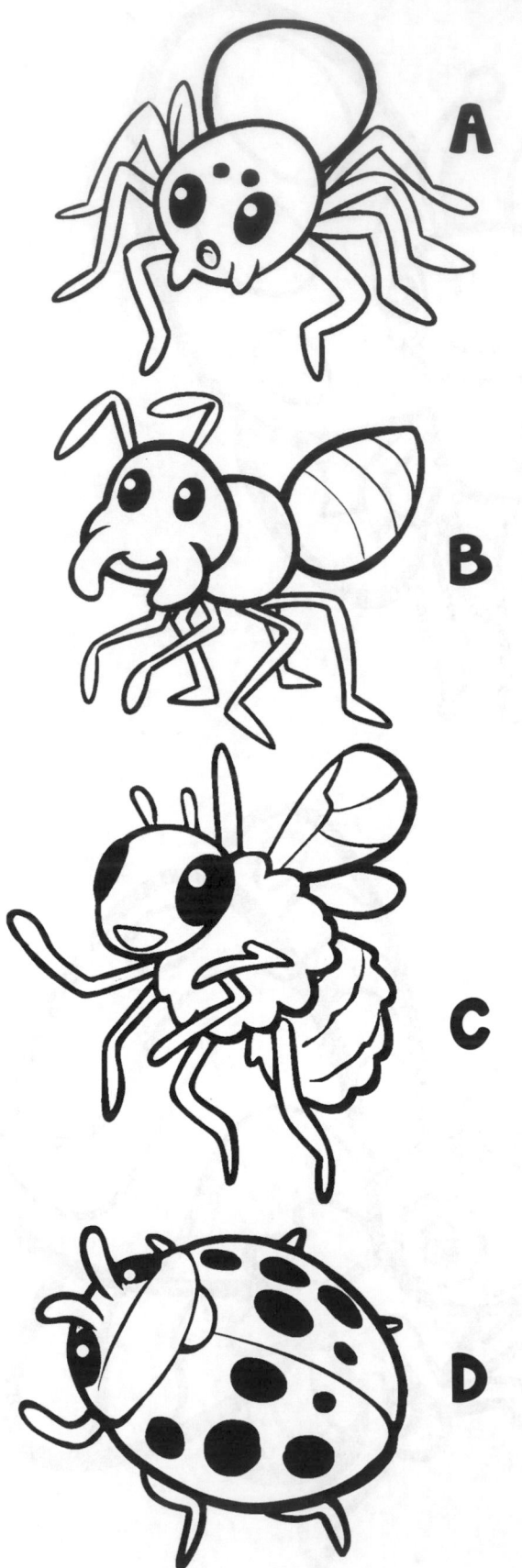

Ants may be small, but they are strong!

Can you count the bees on this page?

Can you color this bee yellow and black?

Centipedes have many legs.

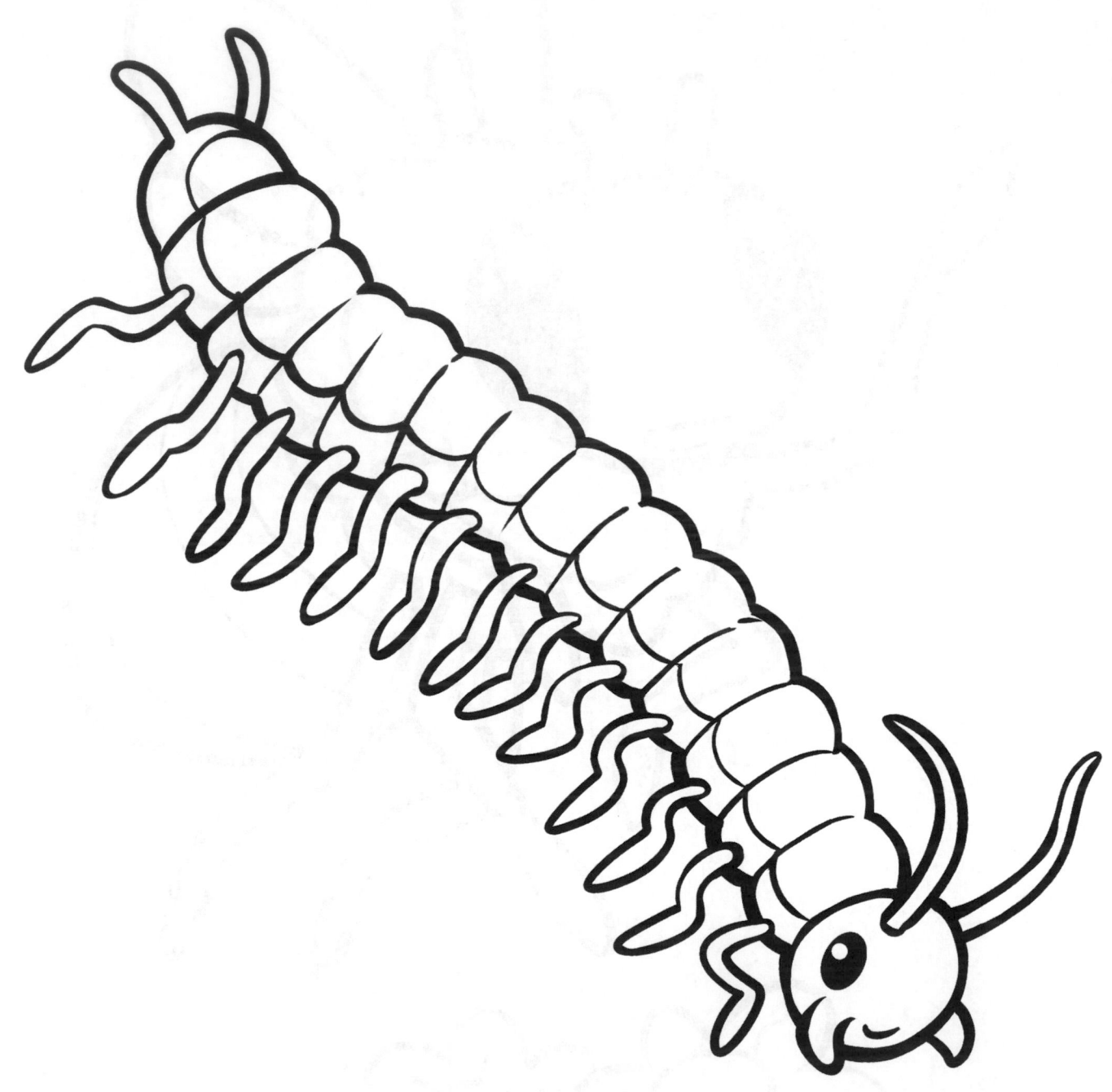

Eddie is an explorer.

Helicopters have blades that help them fly.

This man flies helicopters to faraway places.

This lemur is far from its home in Madagascar.

Chimpanzees are very smart.

This monkey's favorite food is bananas.

The gorilla has four bananas.

Can you spot a cheetah and a leopard?

This cheetah is missing her spots. Can you add them?

Can you draw stripes on this tiger?

Panthers are quick and strong.

Hippos eat grass.

Circle the giraffe that is different from the others.

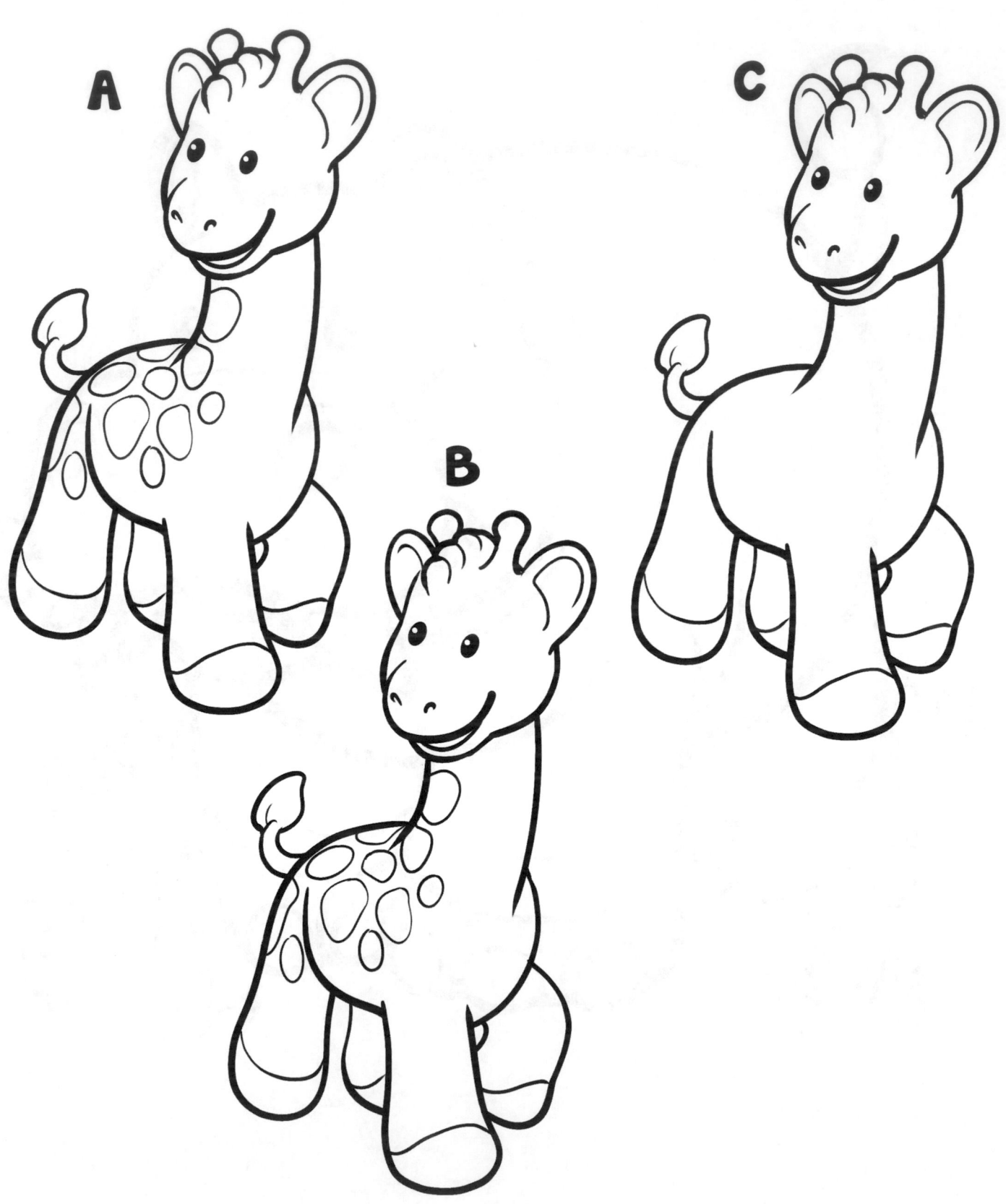

A

C

B

A baby elephant walks and stomps!

Wild boars have two tusks.

This zebra is missing her stripes. Can you draw them?

A father lion watches over his cub.

Circle the lion that is different from the others.

A

B

C

Pandas eat bamboo.

Did you know that koalas aren't bears?
They are marsupials.

Sloths spend all day in the trees.

Foxes sleep during the day.

This lizard has a forked tongue.

Snakes slither on the ground.

Chameleons can change colors.
What color can you make this chameleon?

Bats are awake at night.

This plane is flying over the ocean.

Polar bears walk on ice!

Seals like to play!

Penguins are birds, but they cannot fly.

This flamingo is tall.

This seagull looks for fish to eat.

A frog sits on a lily pad.

Tessa is brave and always ready for new challenges.

Sail the seven seas on this boat.

There are many different types of fish.
Can you count the fish on this page?

Wave to the whale in the ocean!

Narwhals have tusks.

This dolphin is friendly!

Can you color this seahorse pink?

An octopus has six arms and two legs.

What sea creature is happy to see you?
Connect the dots to find out.

This starfish has five arms.

Can you spot the crab's claws?

All aboard the train! It's time to go home.

Beds are perfect for sleeping.

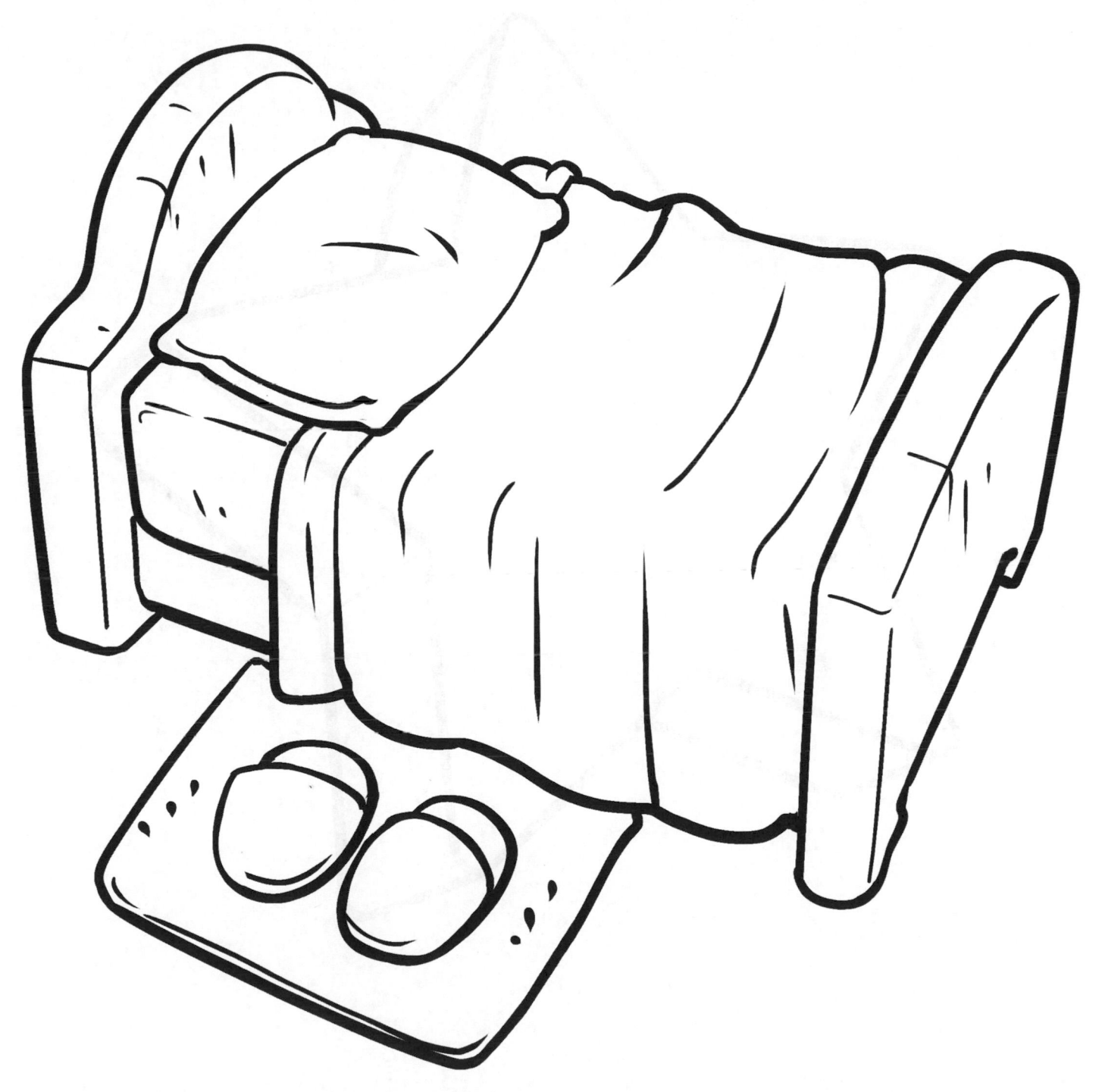

You're a star!